D1267066

WILD WHEELS

LAMBORGHINIS

By Bob Power

Gareth Stevens
Publishing

Please visit our website, www.garethstevens.com. For a free color catalog of all our high-quality books, call toll free 1-800-542-2595 or fax 1-877-542-2596.

Library of Congress Cataloging-in-Publication Data

Power, Bob, 1959-
Lamborghinis / Bob Power.
   p. cm. — (Wild wheels)
Includes index.
ISBN 978-1-4339-5832-8 (pbk.)
ISBN 978-1-4339-5833-5 (6-pack)
ISBN 978-1-4339-5830-4 (library binding)
1. Lamborghini automobile—Juvenile literature. I. Title.
TL215.L33P69 2012
629.222'2—dc22

2011005932

First Edition

Published in 2012 by
Gareth Stevens Publishing
111 East 14th Street, Suite 349
New York, NY 10003

Copyright © 2012 Gareth Stevens Publishing

Designer: Daniel Hosek
Editor: Kristen Rajczak

Photo credits: Cover, backgrounds (cover and interior pages), pp. 1, 20–21, 24–25, 25 (inset) Shutterstock.com; pp. 4–5 Boris Horvat/AFP/Getty Images; pp. 5 (Lamborghini logo), 28–29 David McNew/Getty Images; pp. 6–7 Klemantaski Collection/Hulton Archive/Getty Images; pp. 8–9 Ben Stansall/AFP/Getty Images; p. 9 (Enzo Ferrari) Keystone/Hulton Archive/Getty Images; pp. 10–11 Car Culture/Getty Images; pp. 12–13 Mike Albans/New York Daily News Archive/Getty Images; pp. 14–15, 16–17 Wikimedia Commons; pp. 18–19 Hulton Archive/Getty Images; pp. 22–23 David Hallett/Getty Images; pp. 26–27 Gabriel Bouys/AFP/Getty Images.

Printed in the United States of America

CPSIA compliance information: Batch #CS11GS: For further information contact Gareth Stevens, New York, New York at 1-800-542-2595.

CONTENTS

Words in the glossary appear in **bold** type the first time they are used in the text.

The Perfect Car

Lamborghinis are some of the most famous cars in the world. They're fast and powerful. They look cool, too! Most importantly, Lamborghinis are a joy to drive.

Some car companies put their effort into making race cars. Others want to give buyers the best car for the least money. Lamborghini, however, makes **high-performance** sports cars that are **designed** to be exciting to drive on a regular road.

This Lamborghini was introduced to the public at the Paris Motor Show in 2010.

Lamborghini's logo is a black shield with a gold bull on it. The bull's horns are lowered as if it's about to charge. Bulls are a big part of the company's **identity**.

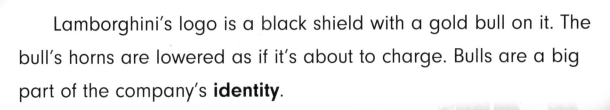

Lamborghini is one of several important sports car manufacturers in Italy. Others include Alfa Romeo, Maserati, and Ferrari. The Italians have a rich history of both car racing and building fine sports cars.

Lamborghini logo

Ferruccio Lamborghini

Ferruccio Lamborghini founded the Lamborghini car company. He was born on April 28, 1916, in Renazzo de Cento, a small village near the Italian city of Bologna. His parents were grape farmers. As a child, Ferruccio was interested in machines. When he was a young man, Italy fought in World War II. Ferruccio joined the army and was sent to the Greek island of Rhodes. There, he spent the war fixing army trucks and other machines.

After the war ended, Ferruccio returned to Italy. He started a business building tractors from pieces of tanks and trucks left behind after the war.

INSIDE THE MACHINE

Two elements affected Ferruccio Lamborghini's choice for his company's logo. One was his **zodiac sign**—Taurus, the bull. The other was his love of bullfighting.

The Lamborghini 350 GTV was the first car to bear the company's bull logo.

From Tractors to Sports Cars

Ferruccio Lamborghini's tractors became a big success. They were considered some of the best and most powerful tractors around. In time, the company began making air conditioners, too. Ferruccio made a lot of money. His new fortune allowed him to buy the sports cars he had loved since childhood. However, Ferruccio wasn't happy with how the cars ran. He decided to make his own sports car.

In 1963, Ferruccio started building a car factory for his new company, Automobili Lamborghini S.p.A. He made sure to hire some of the best engineers in the business.

Ferruccio Lamborghini owned a Ferrari 250 GT similar to this one.

A popular story tells of Ferruccio visiting Ferrari founder Enzo Ferrari to complain. Ferruccio told Enzo that a key part on his Ferrari didn't work well. He said Enzo just laughed at him and told him to go back to working on tractors.

Enzo Ferrari

The GT

In 1963, the Lamborghini company showed off its first **prototype** car at an auto show in Turin, Italy. It was known as the 350 GTV. Even though the car's engine wasn't ready in time for the show, many people were interested in the prototype.

Lamborghini 350 GTs like this one are hard to find today.

Lamborghini reworked the 350 GTV and produced it for public sale in 1964. It was renamed the 350 GT. It had a newly designed V-12 engine. A V-12 engine has two **banks** of 6 **cylinders** set up in a V shape. The engine also had double overhead **cams**. The new system of cams worked fast, which made for a powerful engine.

INSIDE THE MACHINE

Car companies make a prototype when they're thinking of making a new car. Often, only one or two examples are made. Prototypes give possible buyers an idea of what the car will look like. Prototypes are also known as concept cars.

The Miura

The GT was a success. In the following years, Lamborghini made a few improvements to it. Then, in 1966, the company introduced a new Lamborghini to sell alongside it. The new car was called the Miura.

The Miura used a V-12 engine, just as the GT did. However, the position of the engine changed. The GT's engine was in the front, under the car's hood. The Miura had a mid-engine design, which means the engine was in the middle of the car, behind the driver. Mid-engine cars balance better when zipping around corners, which makes them safer to drive.

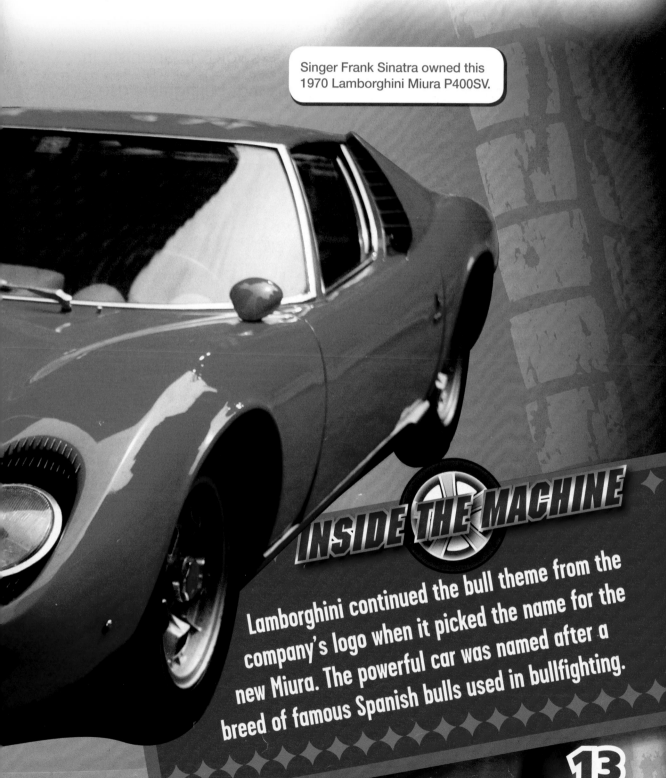

Singer Frank Sinatra owned this 1970 Lamborghini Miura P400SV.

INSIDE THE MACHINE

Lamborghini continued the bull theme from the company's logo when it picked the name for the new Miura. The powerful car was named after a breed of famous Spanish bulls used in bullfighting.

The Espada

The GT and Miura were successes. However, the new car Lamborghini began selling in 1968 was even more popular. The car was named the Espada, which means "sword" in Spanish. In particular, the name applies to the swords that bullfighters use.

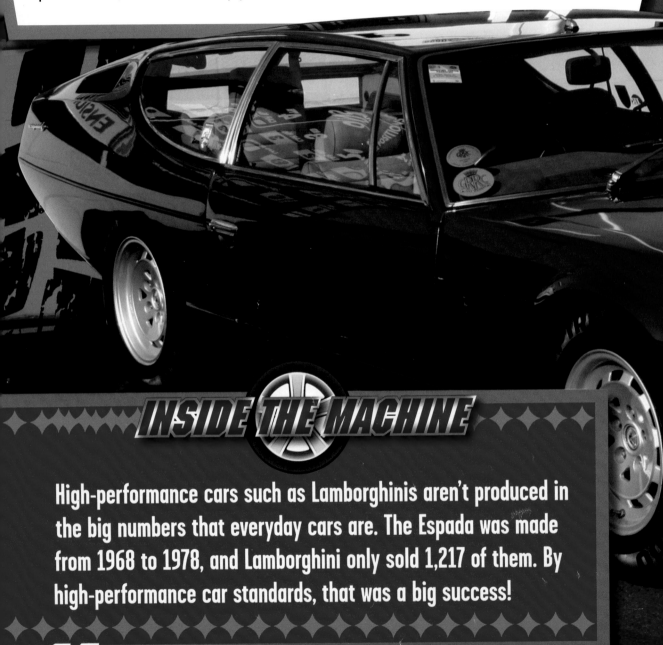

INSIDE THE MACHINE

High-performance cars such as Lamborghinis aren't produced in the big numbers that everyday cars are. The Espada was made from 1968 to 1978, and Lamborghini only sold 1,217 of them. By high-performance car standards, that was a big success!

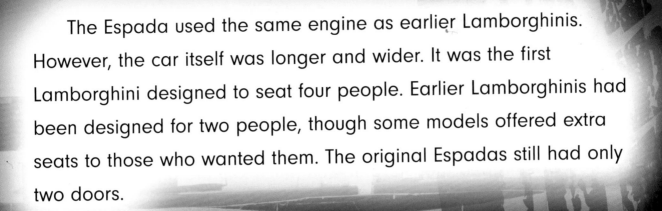

The Espada used the same engine as earlier Lamborghinis. However, the car itself was longer and wider. It was the first Lamborghini designed to seat four people. Earlier Lamborghinis had been designed for two people, though some models offered extra seats to those who wanted them. The original Espadas still had only two doors.

Lamborghini sold three different series of the Espada—the S1, S2, and S3. They all looked similar on the outside.

The Islero and the Jarama

In 1968, Lamborghini decided to update the GT. The new version was named the Islero. It was much like the older model but was redesigned to be more comfortable to drive. The Islero had more room for the driver's legs and head.

Ferruccio Lamborghini himself drove an Islero like this one.

The company introduced a new car called the Jarama in 1970. Like the Islero and the GT before it, the Jarama's engine was in the front. Its mighty V-12 engine produced 350 **horsepower**. In 1973, Lamborghini introduced the Jarama S, also called the GTS. Its engine produced 365 horsepower. The added power came from a new **exhaust system** and other improvements.

INSIDE THE MACHINE

The Islero was named after a powerful bull that killed the bullfighter Manuel Rodriguez in 1947. The Jarama was named after a part of Spain that produced some of the best bulls used in bullfighting.

V-8 Engines

The Urraco was Lamborghini's answer to the smaller, less expensive cars other high-performance carmakers produced during the 1970s. It was the first Lamborghini to have a V-8 engine. In 1970, Lamborghini showed a prototype at the Turin Auto Show. However, it didn't start producing the Urraco until 1973. Urraco, which means "little bull," was named after a famous fighting bull.

This Urraco was a 2+2. It had two seats in the front and two in the back.

The Urraco wasn't the hit it needed to be. Lamborghini tried to improve its position in the car world during the mid-1970s with other models powered by V-8 engines. In 1976, the Silhouette came out, followed by the Jalpa in 1982. Neither was very successful.

INSIDE THE MACHINE

The Silhouette was the first Lamborghini that could be driven as an open-top car. It had a targa top, a hard top with some removable parts. It let Lamborghini drivers feel the wind in their hair as they drove.

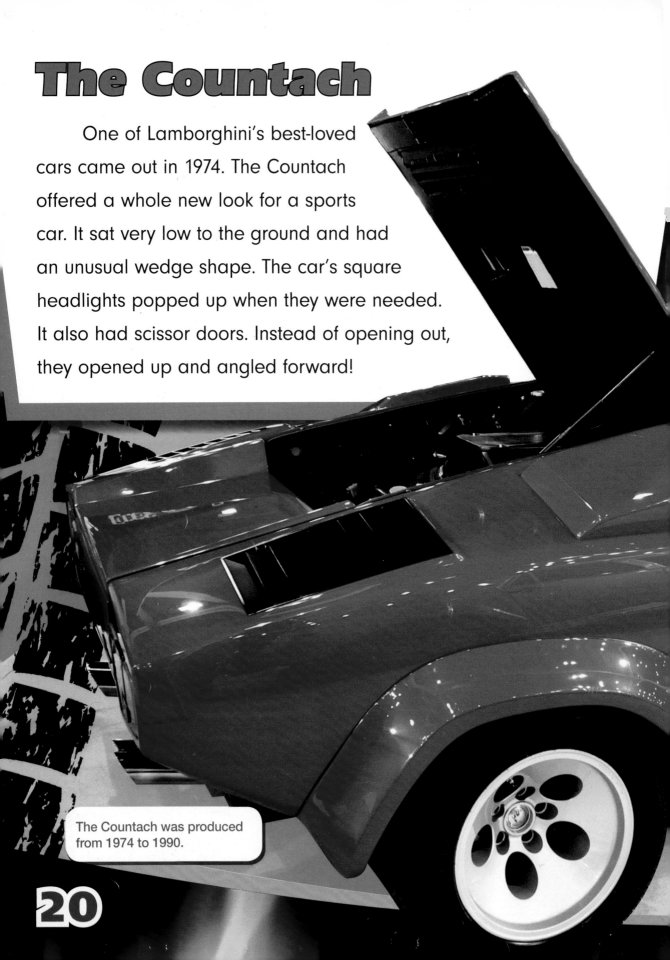

The Countach

One of Lamborghini's best-loved cars came out in 1974. The Countach offered a whole new look for a sports car. It sat very low to the ground and had an unusual wedge shape. The car's square headlights popped up when they were needed. It also had scissor doors. Instead of opening out, they opened up and angled forward!

The Countach was produced from 1974 to 1990.

The Countach had a light body. It was made of lightweight **aluminum** plates mounted on a frame of tubes. Less weight allowed the car to move faster. Its more powerful engine helped it speed along, too. The V-12 produced up to 375 horsepower.

INSIDE THE MACHINE

Ferruccio Lamborghini wanted to make the all-time greatest "supercar." He thought the Countach was so great it couldn't be described in words. In Italian, *countach* means "Wow! Look at this!"

The Diablo

With the coming of the Diablo in 1990, Lamborghini at last had a car that could speed along at more than 200 miles (322 km) per hour. It was named after a bull from a famous bullfight that took place in 1869.

The Diablo was based on the Countach. Its doors opened upward and forward in the same way. It had Lamborghini's famous V-12 engine. It had the Countach's low-riding wedge shape, too. However, the Diablo had a rounder, sleeker look. Lamborghini also used newly invented materials—like aluminum **alloy**—to build it.

INSIDE THE MACHINE

Sports car owners like to drive fast, but driving at high speeds uses up a lot of gas. In order to follow laws about air pollution, the Diablo had to have better **fuel efficiency** than earlier Lamborghinis.

In 1991, the Diablo was the fastest car on the road!

The Murciélago and the Gallardo

In 2001, Lamborghini replaced the Diablo with a new car called the Murciélago. It was less flashy than the Diablo. One of the most eye-catching things about the Murciélago didn't appear until the car was moving fast. Then, **scoops** popped out of the car's sides. These looked cool, but they also served a purpose. They let in air to cool down the engine. Engines get very hot when cars hit high speeds.

Two years later, the company introduced the Lamborghini Gallardo. It had Lamborghini's first 10-cylinder engine, which produced 500 horsepower. The car could go 192 miles (309 km) per hour.

Lamborghini has made and sold more Gallardos than any other kind of car. More than 10,000 Gallardos have been sold since 2003.

Gallardo

Lamborghini worked with fashion designer Versace to create this black-and-white Murciélago.

Cool Cars for Cool People

Lamborghinis' power and good looks have won many fans over the years. Some of these fans are people who have fans of their own. Music stars Justin Bieber and Sean Kingston have been seen driving around Los Angeles, California, in a white Lamborghini Gallardo Spyder. Movie star Nicolas Cage and talk-show host Jay Leno have also driven Lamborghinis.

Lamborghinis also show up in movies. Characters in the 1994 movie *Dumb and Dumber*

A Lamborghini Gallardo Spyder like this one costs more than $200,000!

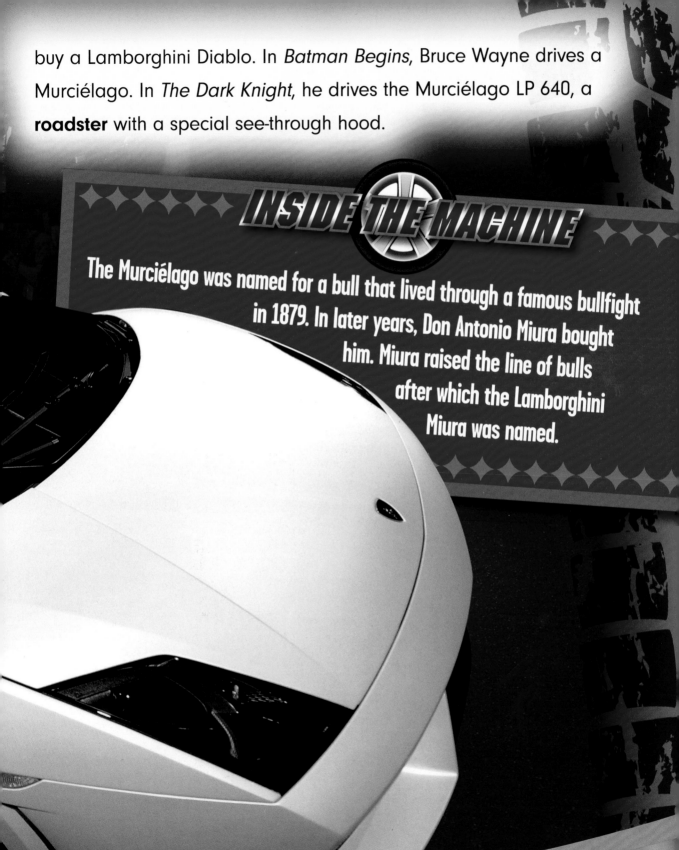

buy a Lamborghini Diablo. In *Batman Begins*, Bruce Wayne drives a Murciélago. In *The Dark Knight*, he drives the Murciélago LP 640, a **roadster** with a special see-through hood.

INSIDE THE MACHINE

The Murciélago was named for a bull that lived through a famous bullfight in 1879. In later years, Don Antonio Miura bought him. Miura raised the line of bulls after which the Lamborghini Miura was named.

What Does the Future Hold?

The Lamborghini company has been through some hard times. There have been years when very few people had money to spare for a high-performance car. The company was bought by another carmaker in the 1970s and has changed hands several times since then. Lamborghini had success in the 2000s, though, when the Murciélago and Gallardo sold well. In 2008, Lamborghini introduced the Reventón. It could reach 211 miles (340 km) per hour!

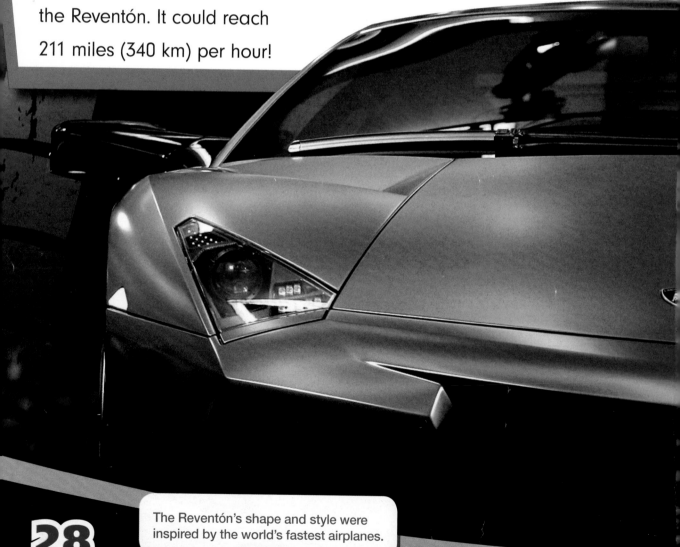

The Reventón's shape and style were inspired by the world's fastest airplanes.

While it's one of the smaller sports-car makers in the world, Lamborghini still competes with Ferrari and Maserati with every new model. The years to come are sure to bring more great Lamborghinis.

INSIDE THE MACHINE

Only 20 Reventóns were produced in 2008. Even though they were very expensive, the cars sold out before Lamborghini had a chance to build them! The cars had a big V-12 engine. They could go from 0 to 60 miles (97 km) per hour in just 3.3 seconds.

Glossary

alloy: a material made of two types of metal, or a metal and a nonmetal, melted together

aluminum: a type of lightweight metal

bank: a group of things that are lined up

cam: an engine part that lets fuel into and exhaust out of an engine

cylinder: the enclosed tube-shaped spaces in an engine where fuel is burned

design: to create the pattern or shape of something

exhaust system: pipes through which gases created by an engine escape

fuel efficiency: the quality of being able to operate using little fuel, or without waste

high-performance: having to do with cars that are made for speed and power

horsepower: the measurement of an engine's power

identity: a set of features that make someone or something special

prototype: the first model on which later models are based

roadster: an open car with just two doors

scoop: an opening on the outside of a car that takes in air for the engine

zodiac sign: a figure that represents qualities of one of 12 specific groups of stars. A person's zodiac sign is based on their birthday.

For More Information

Books

Bradley, Michael. *Lamborghini.* Tarrytown, NY: Marshall Cavendish Benchmark, 2010.

Colson, Rob Scott. *Lamborghini.* New York, NY: PowerKids Press, 2011.

Woods, Bob. *Hottest Sports Cars.* Berkeley Heights, NJ: Enslow Publishers, 2008.

Websites

Automobili Lamborghini S.p.A.
www.lamborghini.com
Learn more about the Lamborghini company and the cars it produces.

LamboCARS.com
www.lambocars.com/lambonews
Keep up with the latest news about Lamborghini on this fan site.

Index